COWBOYS AND COUNTRY
Life in America's Outback

David Ross at the Pitchfork Ranch near Guthrie, Texas, kneels near his campfire outside his range teepee during fall work. "Ross" has been a fixture at the Pitchfork for more than 15 years. He honors tradition and works in the old cowboy way. © ROBB KENDRICK

Published by Purple Coyote Corp. and RANGE magazine
Compiled and edited by C.J. Hadley

COWBOYS AND COUNTRY
LIFE IN AMERICA'S OUTBACK

Publisher/Editor: C.J. Hadley
Senior Writer: Tim Findley
Designer: John Bardwell

Publication of this book was made possible by generous donations from people who care about the American West.

Library of Congress Cataloging-in-Publication Data
Hadley, C.J.
Cowboys and Country:
Life in America's Outback
Caroline Joy Hadley
ISBN 9780974456348
LCCN 2007932750

Published by Purple Coyote Corp. and RANGE magazine, Carson City, Nevada.

$22 U.S.A.
Printed in China

Arizona cowboy Rocky Rains at the Fort
Ranch, Golconda, Nevada. © LARRY TURNER

Great Basin desert that was once the bed of ancient Lake Lahontan, Pershing County, Nevada. © LINDA DUFURRENA

INTRODUCTION

Someday, youngsters yet unborn may pick up this book and allow their imaginations to browse through the images. The West will have changed by then, just as it has generation by generation for centuries, and the young readers may find themselves living in suburbs that were once ranches or in small cities that were once mining camps.

Maybe they will recognize a place, a person, or even a way of life that might still be there beyond the slow reach of history.

Yet the times of our lives leave little chance to linger over a page or two before demanding we move on.

These captured moments in this book express an intimacy with the land and with life that needs not merely to be seen, but to be felt, like dreams you wish to remember.

For those young people especially we hope this book will be not a memorial for what has changed, but a promise for what will still be there if they but search a little more.—*Tim Findley*

"To the complaint, 'There are no people
in these photographs,' I respond, 'There
are always two people: the photographer
and the viewer.'"

Ansel Adams (1902-1984)
American photographer

This little calf is too young to make the long trek to new pasture in southwest Montana. Andy Baldauf will give him a ride in the trailer.
© Cynthia Baldauf

"Far and away the best prize that life offers is the chance to work hard at work worth doing."

Theodore Roosevelt, 26th president of the United States (1901-1909) speech in New York, September 7, 1903

Busi family gather cattle for calf marking and branding, Jackson, California.
© Larry Angier

Repairs are a regular part of a cowboy's job: two to work, one to advise, Beaverhead County, Montana.
© CYNTHIA BALDAUF

Catching a horse from the remuda, Pitchfork Ranch, West Texas. Each Pitchfork cowpuncher has a string of half a dozen horses, some broke, some green.
© Bob Moorhouse

Cowpuncher shoes one of his horses. There is so much country to work at the Pitchfork in West Texas, "some hard as hell," a fresh mount is always needed.
© Bob Moorhouse

Ranch mom Kelly Kirkpatrick performs two jobs with ease, Bacon Ranch, Wise River, Montana. © CYNTHIA BALDAUF

Buster Dufurrena, Dufurrena Sheep Ranch, Humboldt County, Nevada, separates lambs from ewes so they can be weighed on the scales and classed. © LINDA DUFURRENA

Megan Dufurrena helps her father Hank with an orphan lamb, Lovely Valley, Nevada. © LINDA DUFURRENA

Jefferson River country, Montana.
© DAVID MUENCH

Black clouds, lightning and rain over Comanche National Grassland, Colorado.
© LARRY ANGIER

"I love to think of nature as an unlimited
broadcasting station, through which God speaks
to us every hour, if we will only tune in."

George Washington Carver (1864-1943)
American botanist and farmer

Dick Bass from Owyhee, left, and friend Payne enjoy the Jordan Valley, Oregon, Big Loop Rodeo.
© LARRY ANGIER

"My best friend is the one who brings out the best in me."

Henry Ford (1863-1947)
American automobile manufacturer

Amanda Wiggins and a trusty companion at the Roaring Springs Ranch along Oregon's Catlow Rim. Amanda trains and breaks horses for the ranch.
© LARRY TURNER

Buckaroo sisters Maura and Ricarda Bradbury of Plush, Oregon, take a
break after horse chores at the Bradbury Ranch. © LARRY TURNER

Black Rock Desert to
Sentinel Peak with Pine
Forest Mountains in
background, Humboldt
County, Nevada.
© LINDA DUFURRENA

Poppies bloom and bare
oaks bud in late winter on a
hillside near the Mokelumne
River in the Sierra foothills,
Jackson, California.
© LARRY ANGIER

John and Sue House
walk to their barn
during a winter storm
in Poe Valley, Oregon.
© LARRY TURNER

"A good marriage is one which allows for change and growth in the individuals and in the way they express their love."

Pearl S. Buck (1892-1973)
American novelist

Newlyweds Norman and Sue Sharp from Railroad Valley take time for a quick photo with their dogs and the waxing moon. They are enjoying sister-in-law Lina Sharp's annual Blue Eagle Ranch party in August in central Nevada. Norman owns the Sharp Ranch at Nyala.

© LARRY ANGIER

Leppy (orphan) lambs in the pen, Dufurrena Ranch, Denio, Nevada. © LARRY ANGIER

Moving a band of sheep to
new ground in the high brush
country of northern Nevada.
© LINDA DUFURRENA

This colorful band of bucking horses was raised on the Hirschy Ranch in the Big Hole Valley, Montana. They are on a break from rodeo work.
© Cynthia Baldauf

Horse kiss,
Fredericksburg, Texas.
© Larry Turner

This two-year-old draft horse is a little touchy during hookup to the hay sled. Dan Coon uses a broom to desensitize it, Wisdom, Montana.
© Cynthia Baldauf

Molly Knudtsen, Grass Valley Ranch,
central Nevada. © REED BINGHAM

"To be 70 years young is sometimes
far more cheerful and hopeful than to
be 40 years old."

Oliver Wendell Holmes Sr.
U.S. author and physician (1809-1894)

Henry Gray, rancher, Arizona, 1970.
© WILLIAM ALBERT ALLARD

"In every walk with nature one receives far more than he seeks."

John Muir (1838-1914)
Naturalist

A late fall storm over the Bilk Creek Mountains, north of Winnemucca, Nevada. Cowboys must battle droughts, floods, blizzards and dust storms. The rest of the time, they complain about the weather. Why give up on a good fight when you've got one? © Linda Dufurrena

No full service here in Jackson, Montana.
© Cynthia Baldauf

Cannery rows. © Jeanne Sharp Howerton

The old store and bus depot in Orla, Texas, population two, is kept afloat by ranchers and oil drillers. © Larry Angier

Sierra Madre Mountains, northern Santa Barbara County, California.
© MARC MUENCH

Spring runoff, Jackson Mountains. "It is my spring ritual to gather a few desert peach blossoms and one of my favorite places is the west side of the Jackson Mountains in Humboldt County, Nevada. Usually there are some nice small creeks that flow in the spring from snowmelt."
© LINDA DUFURRENA

"Tug on anything at all and you'll find it connected to everything else in the universe."

John Muir (1838-1914)
Naturalist

Doug Groves of the T Lazy S Ranch in Battle Mountain, Nevada, looks for strays in high, cold country.
© C.J. Hadley

"I have friends in overalls whose friendship I would not swap for the favor of the kings of the world."

Thomas Edison (1847-1931)
American inventor

Buckaroo stands beside his mount at the old MC Ranch outside Adel, Oregon.
© Larry Turner

Cowboys are out for months with the wagon, Pitchfork Ranch, West Texas. During bad weather, chuck is served under canvas. © Bob Moorhouse

Jon Griggs, manager of Maggie Creek Ranch near Elko, Nevada, is a well-respected buckaroo who understands the balance of managing a large ranch, dealing with the blows that Mother Nature throws his way, and the ever-changing rules of the federal government. He is photographed in the window frame of one of the historic barns at the ranch.

TINTYPE © ROBB KENDRICK

These cowpunchers were photographed at the JA Ranch near Clarendon, Texas. From left, Rhett Cauble, Buck McLain and R.D. Horn lean against one of the historic barns near ranch headquarters. The JA was founded by Charles Goodnight, whose family still owns the ranch.

TINTYPE © ROBB KENDRICK

"Freedom is never more than one generation away from extinction. We didn't pass it to our children in the bloodstream. It must be fought for, protected, and handed on for them to do the same, or one day we will spend our sunset years telling our children and our children's children what it was once like in the United States where men were free."

Ronald Reagan (1911-2004), 40th president of the United States, 1981-1989

Ten-year-old Garret Gillmore of George, Washington.
© LARRY ANGIER

A large contingent of horsemen help protest the 2001 water cutoff to family farmers and ranchers in Klamath Basin on the Oregon/California line. They are riding to the headgates to show their support for the rural people affected by the federal action that left crops and stock high and dry.
© LARRY TURNER

"There can be no fifty-fifty Americanism in this country; there is room here for only 100 percent. Americanism, only for those who are Americans and nothing else."

Theodore Roosevelt (1858-1919) *26th president of the United States, 1901-1909*

Oregon buckaroo and horse trainer Odie Wright and his 17-hand Percheron, Titan.

© LARRY TURNER

Navajo matriarch Alice Begay and great-grandchildren travel with her son Rev. Darrellson Begay and family to visit Goosenecks State Park, Utah. They live in Gallup, New Mexico. © LARRY ANGIER

Big Loop Rodeo cowboy poet Toni Maguiere, Jordan Valley, Oregon. © LARRY ANGIER

Seth Watrous with his Sunday-go-to-meetin' wild rag. Seth works for Oregon's Ponderosa Ranch. At 33, he has three children and has buckarooed in four states. © LARRY TURNER

"There is nothing wrong with America that the faith, love of freedom, intelligence and energy of her citizens cannot cure."

Dwight D. Eisenhower (1890-1969)
34th president of the United States, 1953-1961

High desert buckaroo DaeNell Douglas of Roaring Springs Ranch, Fields, Oregon.
© LARRY TURNER

Gary and Terri Poggio take shelter in a stock trailer during a late winter storm. They are helping with spring branding at the Busi Ranch in the Sierra foothills near Jackson, California. It's been a tradition since Gold Rush days for old-time families to gather and help one another with the brandings. They work and socialize, renewing their ties to one another. © LARRY ANGIER

Girl in canvas teepee at a cowboy music gathering in Elko, Nevada.
© C.J. Hadley

Virginia Stanford, Jordan Valley, Oregon.
© Larry Angier

Tim Crutcher, Indian cowboy with wild rag at the Rome Station Café in Rome, Oregon. © Larry Angier

Early morning is the best time: a whole new day is out there for young cowboys raring to go, eager to find out how much was learned yesterday. These Spanish Ranch cowboys have wrangled horses, eaten breakfast, and are ready to ride before sunup, northeastern Nevada. © C.J. HADLEY

"America lives in the heart of every man everywhere who wishes to find a region where he will be free to work out his destiny as he chooses."

Woodrow Wilson (1856-1924), 28th president of the United States, 1913-1921

Calling in extra troops. Dogs help turn a wayward calf back to the corrals at the Cuneo Ranch branding, Plymouth, California. © Carolyn Fox

Jess White's buckaroo camp,
Owyhee Desert, Oregon.
© Pam White

"Lonely roads through western states are like the rivers and trails that carried the first pioneers. You roll along, held in the traveled course, and yet your imagination wanders to the hills and the canyons. Just beyond that mountain, or perhaps far into the shadows of that crease, maybe even in the shelter near a distantly seen meadow, is there perhaps a place seldom, if ever, visited by man? Good sense tells you, no. But still…if there was only enough time…."

Tim Findley, RANGE magazine

Thunderstorm along U.S. Highway 380,
Jornada Del Muerto, New Mexico.
© LARRY ANGIER

"Half our life is spent trying to find something to do with the time we have rushed through life trying to save."

Will Rogers (1879-1935)
American actor and humorist

Stan Kendall in the Miner's Club,
Mountain City, Nevada, 1979.
© WILLIAM ALBERT ALLARD

"After you have exhausted what there is in business, politics, conviviality, and so on—have found that none of these finally satisfy, or permanently wear—what remains? Nature remains."

Walt Whitman (1819-1892)
American poet

Claret-cup hedgehog cactus.
© DOUG SOKELL, TOM STACK & ASSOCIATES

Oaks in springtime,
Picacho Pass
country, California.
© DAVID MUENCH

Cameron Johnston loses his grip during junior steer riding at the
Jordan Valley Big Loop Rodeo in Oregon. © LARRY ANGIER

"When you play, play hard;
when you work, don't play at all."

Theodore Roosevelt (1858-1919)
26th president of the United States,
1901-1909

"The Big Loop" horse roping at the rodeo in Jordan Valley, Oregon. © LARRY ANGIER

In early spring, cowboys push cattle to new feed ground for the Quinn River Crossing Ranch in northern Nevada.
© LINDA DUFURRENA

"The story of the West—past, present, and future—is in the water. Even in the 'driest state' of Nevada where rivers flow to the Great Basin and vanish into deep land-locked lakes or shallow swampy 'sinks' as if still trying to replenish the vast inland sea that once was there. The great mystery is that it still exists, far below the surface in most places, but still there as a great reservoir marking time by millennia."

Tim Findley, RANGE magazine

Likely, California, rancher Rod Flournoy considers spreading irrigation water an art, not a job for unskilled labor. © Barney Nelson

Brian Oneto, son Ben and daughter Sarah at their ranch in Drytown, California. The dog Zeke is a flat-coated retriever. © LARRY ANGIER

"We cannot always build the future for our youth, but we can build our youth for the future."

Franklin D. Roosevelt (1882-1945)
32nd president of the United States, 1933-1945

Crystalin Chrisensen from McMinnville, Oregon, with daughter Gaden and dog Gus. © LARRY ANGIER

It's an 18-mile trip to summer cow camp for the Petersons. Harold Peterson and Jon King walk out the kinks with baby Malcolm during lunch break, Jackson, Montana.
© CYNTHIA BALDAUF

Kids with puppies at the "Buckaroo Fest" ranch rodeo in Gardnerville, Nevada.
© CAROLYN FOX

"Some kids will become astronauts and some will become rock stars; some will be corporate executives and some will be architects. But I'll bet all of them at some point wanted to be a cowboy."

Tim Findley, RANGE magazine

Christian Lacy, age 3, "hit the ground wanting to be a cowboy just like his dad" at the o6 Ranch in West Texas. Still wearing a diaper, he is already gifted at coiling a rope. © DIANE LACY

Cousins Luke and Alfred Peterson try out saddle-bronc moves while safely on the ground, Jackson, Montana. © CYNTHIA BALDAUF

"My mother had a great deal of trouble with me,
but I think she enjoyed it."

Mark Twain (1835-1910)
American writer

Hannabell Barbee from Skiatook, Oklahoma, is proud of her taco hat at the Jordan Valley Big Loop Rodeo in Oregon.
© LARRY ANGIER

Bree Coon and her cousin are keeping the saddle warm for dad between rounds in the sorting pen, Wisdom, Montana. © CYNTHIA BALDAUF

Troy Kirkpatrick will learn the value of planning ahead after he throws this loop, Big Hole Valley, Montana.
© CYNTHIA BALDAUF

"There is joy in work. There is no happiness except
in the realization that we have accomplished something."

Henry Ford (1863-1947)
American automobile manufacturer

Buckaroo John Schutte
owns cattle in Bruneau,
Idaho, and in Casa
Grande, Arizona.
A great roper, John
helps the PX crew
brand cattle on
Hendricks Creek near
Wildhorse, Nevada.
© CHRISSY KING

Arambel Ranch moves 10,000 sheep in five bands. Each is accompanied by a Nepalese sheepherder, a wagon, two horses, four or five herd dogs and several large, white guard dogs to protect the flocks from predators, including wolves. The bands travel a day apart, 200 miles from their winter range in northern Colorado to their summer range in Wyoming. The trek takes weeks and includes river crossings and all kinds of weather, including blizzards. © CHARLES W. GUILDNER

Lynn Ness, buckaroo cowboss for Simplot, enjoys branding cattle with his crew at Sheep Creek in southwest Idaho.
© CHRISSY KING

There is nothing
so sweet as the
lush grass on the
sides of the
irrigation ditches,
Beaverhead
County, Montana.
© Cynthia Baldauf

These white fillies are Grey Eagle daughters, 2006 Cayuse Ranch foals.
Their sire is a striking grulla and they look like ghosts in a herd of duns. © Lucia Roda

"I can always tell which is the front end of a horse,
but beyond that, my art is not above the ordinary."

Mark Twain (1835-1910)
American writer

Minden Ranch Rodeo calf roping at Douglas County Fairgrounds, Gardnerville, Nevada. This rodeo features working cowboys and real-life ranch events. © LARRY ANGIER

Jesse White heels a steer while practicing with his son Tim in preparation for the Jordan Valley Big Loop Rodeo. They are from Rome, Oregon, and came in second in the big loop and team roping—the two events they entered. © LARRY ANGIER

"Cowboys are certainly extremely good riders. As a class they have no superiors."

Theodore Roosevelt, 26th president of the United States, 1901-1909, from "Ranch Life and the Hunting-Trail," 1896

"The clearest way into the Universe is through a forest wilderness."

John Muir (1838-1914), American naturalist

California oaks, nature's rooftop. © Larry Angier

After a cattle roundup on the ranch of Giles and Delta Dalby near Post, Texas, Justin Johnson passes the time in a tack shed while waiting for his father to return.
© Joel Sartore

Grandma Nin plays horse for cowboy Ned who ropes brother Evan, Whitefish Lake, Montana. © Suzanne Lyon Eyre

Chance Story is safely protected in a mineral tub while his mother is a few feet away doing chores, Arrow Ranch, Wisdom, Montana.
© Cynthia Baldauf

"Humor is the great thing, the saving thing. The minute it crops up, all our irritations and resentments slip away and a sunny spirit takes their place."

Mark Twain (1835-1910)
American writer

Moving cattle to fresh feed across the Owyhee Desert on the Idaho/Nevada line.
© C.J. Hadley

"Do not hire a man who does your work for money, but him who does it for love of it."

Henry David Thoreau (1817-1862)
American writer

YP Ranch camp cook pretends to dish up kitty for lunch, northeastern Nevada. © C.J. HADLEY

Jim Bob Waldon holds about 50 mares, ready to
be vaccinated at the Quien Sabe Ranch outside
Channing, Texas. © Con Haffmans

Denny Rechel, buckaroo boss, brands some "late ones" at K.C. Livestock outside Fallon, Nevada. He and his wife Kim run a custom hay operation.
© CON HAFFMANS

Brent Smith of Fallon, Nevada, has cowboyed all over the West and also works as a preacher. "God created truth and honesty in the horse," he says, "and man now has to learn that truth and honesty in that horse."
© CON HAFFMANS

One of rancher Geri Byrne's border collies takes a break on a tractor seat in Modoc County, California. © LARRY TURNER

"A dog is the only thing on earth that loves you more than he loves himself."

Josh Billings, pen name of American humorist Henry Wheeler Shaw (1818-1885)

Adria Schmitt
and her dog,
Monroe, Oregon.
© Larry Angier

7L Ranch, northeast of Casper, Wyoming. © Doug Cooper

"I like pigs. Dogs look up to us. Cats look down on us. Pigs treat us as equals."

Sir Winston Churchill
(1874-1965);
British statesman;
prime minister,
1940-45, 1951-55

Slumbering sows take a break at the end of a long county-fair weekend in Burns, Oregon.
© LINDA DUFURRENA

Hogan School is an old one-room schoolhouse with its grounds now used by cattle.
It is on a desolate road leading to Red Lodge, Montana. © Linda Ellwein

"The school is the last expenditure upon which America should be willing to economize."

Franklin D. Roosevelt (1882-1945)
32nd president of the United States, 1933-1945

Ellsworth Rural School (2003), Sheridan County, Nebraska, was organized February 19, 1896. Previous to the present building, two other schoolhouses were used; one sod and one frame. Mr. and Mrs. Walter Wightman contributed the land for the present school building which was built about 1932. From left to right, on park bench: Stephanie Graham (school board), Dave Andrick (teacher), LeaAnn Buskirk (teacher), Melody Strasburger (traveling music teacher). On the merry-go-round, left to right: Jessie Schwanebeck, Shae Brennan, Ty Grimes, Alisha Conner, Jake Schwanebeck, Josh Conner, Tyler Nielson, Danielle Brennan, Shelby Grimes, Hazy Nielson. © CHARLES W. GUILDNER

Snow geese, Bosque del Apache National Widlife Refuge, New Mexico. © CYNTHIA DELANEY

"Man's heart away from nature becomes hard."

Luther Standing Bear (1869-1939)
Oglala Sioux chief, 1905-1939

Organ-pipe cactus.
© DOUG SOKELL,
TOM STACK & ASSOCIATES

Saguaro, Organ Pipe
Cactus National
Monument,
southern Arizona.
© DOUG SOKELL,
TOM STACK & ASSOCIATES

Doug Young keeps an eye on the herd during the Dry Head Ranch fall horse drive across Montana's Pryor Mountains. © Guy de Galard

"I don't pity any man who does hard work worth doing. I admire him. I pity the creature who does not work, at whichever end of the social scale he may regard himself as being."

Theodore Roosevelt (1858-1919)
26th president of the United States, 1901-1909

Joe Kingen and Jason Ott from Crain, Oregon, at the scale house in Jordan Valley.
© Larry Angier

Doug Groves, cowboss of the T Lazy S Ranch near Battle Mountain, Nevada, gets ready to rope horses from the cavvy for the buckaroo crew. Each of the buckaroos has a string of several horses and they select one daily, based on the type of work to be done.
© C.J. HADLEY

Sue Fairclo House feeds alfalfa to her cattle on a winter Oregon day.
© LARRY TURNER

About 400 head of cattle en route to the Livestock Events
Center in Reno, Nevada, for the Reno Rodeo.
© Jessica Brandi Lifland

Spring branding at Spring Valley
Ranch, Boise, Idaho, is holding on
against mounting populations and
subdivision-development pressure.
© Linda Ellwein

Cowboy Steve Marriot competes at the Minden Ranch Rodeo in Gardnerville, Nevada. © LARRY ANGIER

"There has never yet been a man in our history who led a life of ease whose name is worth remembering."

Theodore Roosevelt (1858-1919)
26th president of the United States,
1901-1909

Dave Thoresen, out with the Spanish Ranch wagon, gathering cattle for branding in the Tuscarora Mountains of northeastern Nevada. The cowboys break camp and move until "every square mile of the Spanish Ranch has been trotted upon." © C.J. HADLEY

Amos with his father Cliff Peterson from Wauna, Washington. © Larry Angier

"Build me a son, O Lord, who will be strong enough to know when he is weak, and brave enough to face himself when he is afraid, one who will be proud and unbending in honest defeat, and humble and gentle in victory."

Douglas MacArthur (1880-1964)
American general

Cowgirl Meggie
Mackenzie from
Baker City,
Oregon.
© LARRY ANGIER

A fiery sunset over the Pine Forest Mountains, the backyard for Dufurrena Sheep and Cattle Company, northern Nevada.
© Linda Dufurrena

Reflections at sunrise in alkaline Middle Lake, Surprise Valley, California. The usually dry lake was photographed at the end of a seven-year drought. In prehistoric times, the lake was 500 feet deep. © Michael Sykes

"Sunsets are like snowflakes. One is never just like another. That's why the best of them are always worth pausing to watch melt away as something that can never quite be seen again."

Tim Findley, RANGE magazine

Chain-fruit cholla and saguaro cacti, Sonoran Desert, southern Arizona.
© DOUG SOKELL, TOM STACK & ASSOCIATES

Saguaro fruit in the Arizona desert. The night-blooming flowers appear in April or May and the juicy red fruit matures by late June. © Doug Sokell, Tom Stack & Associates

Dufurrena Ranch, Humboldt County, Nevada. Hank Dufurrena helps his son Zack with his saddle after branding. © LINDA DUFURRENA

"I have found the best way to give advice
to your children is to find out what they want
and then advise them to do it."

Harry S. Truman (1884-1972)
33rd president of the United States, 1945-1953

Mel Ellwein, boss of Lazy E Ranch and member of Pass Creek Grazing Association in Mackay, Idaho, stops to have a quick meeting with his president, Basco, and his line staff on the ground while cows are moved to new pasture. © LINDA ELLWEIN

On a back road in central Utah, this sheep operation is busy
preparing for shipping. This hired man is well skilled at the art of
handling a band of about a thousand sheep. © LINDA ELLWEIN

This is rush hour for Bud, an 11-year-old red heeler/Catahoola.
He herds cattle at the End of the Trail Ranch outside Helena, Montana.
Bud is fearless and very proud of his mud line. © SANDY OWENS

Chilean buckaroo
Dany Oyarzun at
Jim Cockrell's
Double Bar X ranch
in Lake City,
California.
© LARRY TURNER

Regina Brush gets her hair rinsed by Kat Grashuis after a long, hot day in the saddle. © Jessica Brandi Lifland

This cowboy drove over 300 miles to help move cattle across Nevada's high desert.

"We are all here for a spell;
get all the good laughs you can."

Will Rogers (1879-1935)
American humorist

A couple enjoys old-time country music during a hoedown in Cedarville, California.
© LARRY TURNER

Cattle in the Valley of the Moon along the Reese River in Lander County, Nevada. The mountains are the Shoshone Range.
© LARRY ANGIER

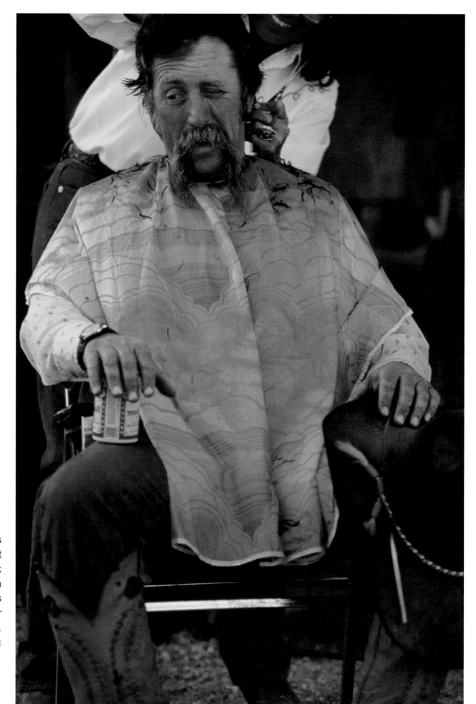

Billy Mitchell gets an outdoor haircut during a break from cattle work on Dave Fisher's Shield F Ranch near Daggett, California.
© JOEL SARTORE

A good drink of good water, near Albion, Idaho. © GWEN MONTGOMERY

"If you would seek to have a sense of time,
dip your hand in the flow of a stream melting
away the winter and see if you can catch it."

Tim Findley, RANGE magazine

Burros on the Black Rock Desert in northwestern Nevada. © DUANE MCGARVA

"In wilderness I sense the miracle of life, and behind it our scientific accomplishments fade to trivia."

Charles Lindbergh (1902-1974)
American aviator

The sawtooths of the Jackson Mountains, Nevada. © LINDA DUFURRENA

Feeding cattle using draft horses and sleigh, Lamoille, Nevada. © PAULA KRUGERUD

"Whose woods these are I think I know.
His house is in the village though;
He will not see me stopping here
To watch his woods fill up with snow."

Robert Frost (1874-1963)
from "Stopping by Woods on a Snowy Evening"

ZX Ranch buckaroo Josh Ashford pauses during a 2,000-head cattle drive from winter range to spring range. The ZX headquarters are in Paisley, Oregon.
© LARRY TURNER

Each buckaroo at the ZX Ranch has a string of half a dozen horses. With the huge circles they make on the desert, often at a long trot, good shoes and good horses are critical. The ranch runs cattle on more than two million acres, with headquarters in Paisley, Oregon. © C.J. HADLEY

Buckaroos and cattle on the move in the sagebrush country of northern Nevada and southern Idaho's high desert. © C.J. HADLEY

Entrance to Vaira Ranch near Drytown, California. © Larry Angier

PUBLISHED BY PURPLE COYOTE CORP.

AND RANGE MAGAZINE

1-800-RANGE-4-U $22 U.S.A.